Simple
Printmaking
with Children

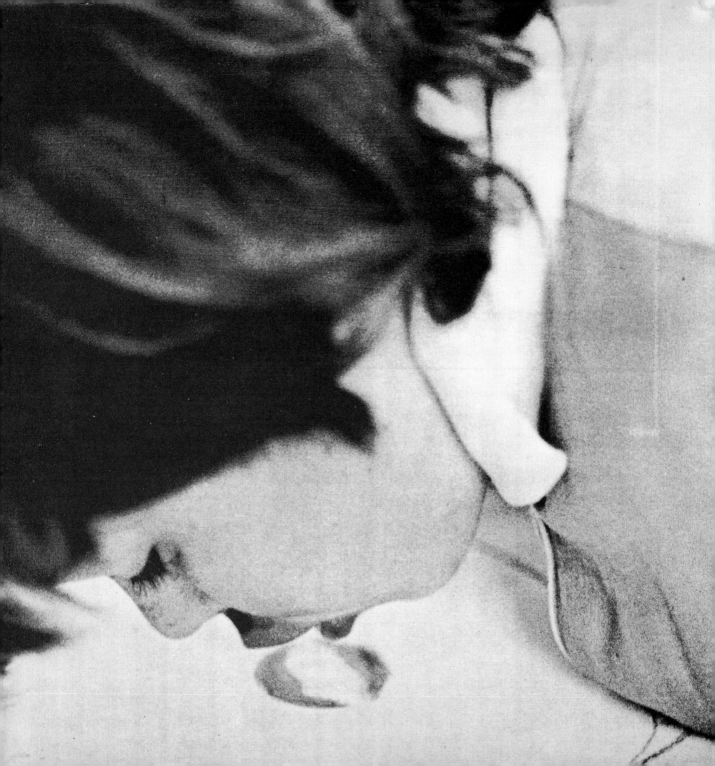

Harvey Daniels and Silvie Turner

Simple Printmaking

with Children

VNR Van Nostrand Reinhold Company
New York · Cincinnati · Toronto · London · Melbourne

For Zoë Daniels

Frontispiece.
Fig. 1. Joseph Anthony using lipstick to print his lips for detail of his self portrait.

Library of Congress Catalog Card Number 78-165923
ISBN 0442 01986 6

Designed by Rod Josey
This book is set in Monophoto Apollo and is printed in Great Britain by Jolly & Barber Ltd., Rugby and bound by the Ferndale Book Company

Published by Van Nostrand Reinhold Company, Inc., 450 West 33rd Street, New York, N.Y. 10001 and Van Nostrand Reinhold Company Ltd., Windsor House, 46 Victoria Street, London SW1

Published simultaneously in Canada by Van Nostrand Reinhold Company Ltd.

16 15 14 13 12 11 10 9 8 7 6 5 4 3 2 1

CONTENTS

INTRODUCTION

'We have persistently taught art as a craft or skill which can be mastered by a talented minority. Art is a human reaction to environment and man's existence. We must therefore cease seeing art teaching as a means of passing on a mystique to those born with talent. Our aim is to provide a visual education, and in the process develop perception and sensitivity.'
Peter Thursby, Hele's School, Exeter.

'My occasional experiences in showing children how to make a print have convinced me that it is practicable and very constructive. They are fascinated and stimulated by this new experience. Printmaking develops manual skill, co-ordination, visual perception, and discipline in procedures.'
Gabor Peterdi.

This book is a collection of prints, the majority of which are by children. It is divided into two volumes to separate the very simple from the more complicated ways of making a print. In the first volume, *Simple Printmaking*, simple methods of making prints without the use of a press are described. The techniques require very little specialist equipment and knowledge, and can be used by children from the age of three upwards (see Fig. 5). The second volume, *Exploring Printmaking*, includes the use of different types of presses and machinery, and more sophisticated methods of making a print.

We have not given detailed explanations of how to carry out very complex methods of printmaking as specialist books are available on all of these subjects. These are listed in the Bibliography in *Exploring Printmaking*. All the methods have, however, been classified into groups; and though

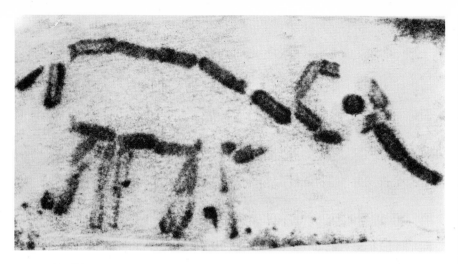

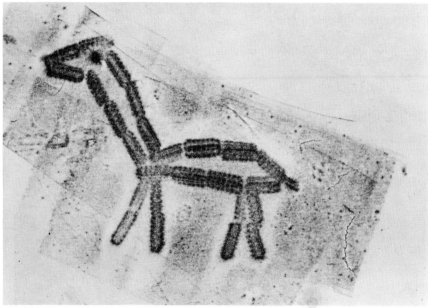

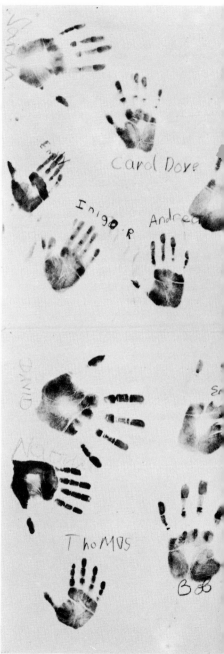

Above. Figs. 3-4. 'Animals'.
David Pauder, age 9. An inked roller was used on the top of the paper, metal objects were placed underneath. (Saturday morning children's classes, Ohio University. Instructor Melody Weiler.)

Right. Fig. 5. 'Handprints'.
Relief prints with signatures made by children, aged 3-14, as a signing-in gesture and direct introduction to relief printing on a three-day course. (East Sussex County Art Centre, Lewes.)

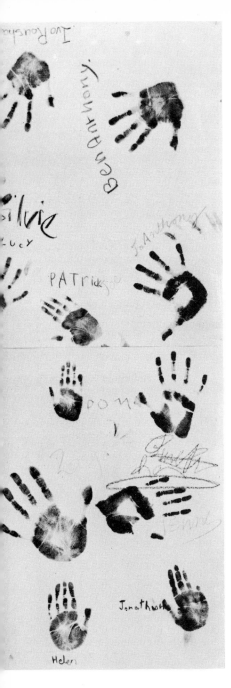

Fig. 6. 'Untitled'.
Ronald Brayley, age 8. A lithograph drawn on a stone.

one particular method may fit into more than one group, it will have been mentioned only in the group in which its main characteristics lie.

When we set out to write this book, we began by relating various methods to various ages. However we found that young children tackled complicated methods quite easily (see Fig. 6) and that older children often preferred simple methods (see Fig. 10). We decided therefore to divide up the chapters into groups of related print methods. The chapter on Transfer Printing, for example, includes monoprinting, transfer drawing and printing, rubbing, marbling and decalcomania.

Particular images recur throughout the book showing the different ways in which they can be printed; the hand has been used as an example in many chapters. Fig. 47 shows a handstamp, and Fig. 136, a stencilled hand. The characteristic

of the specific method that is being used is important. Each print method has its own peculiar mark which often cannot be made by any other activity. Fig. 7 shows a relief print taken from a slice of bread. Whether drawn, painted or photographed, the piece of bread would not have the detail or appearance that printing has given it.

The traditional role of print making is often regarded in schools as a craft-orientated or narrow specialist subject. One aim in writing this book is to indicate the wide range of possibilities that are available to children within the various printmaking methods. The prints shown in this book have not been selected because they are minor works of art, but because they are pointers to processes and ideas. We hope that they show not only the reasons for using different print methods, but also various ways in which the problems of

Left. Fig. 7. 'Bread'.
Phillipa Hughes, age 15. Relief print of
found object.

Right. Fig. 8. Dom, age 5, printing a sheep
by repeatedly stamping a wooden letter on
a painted green background. This involved
only the use of paper, water-based paint
and the letter.

visual research can be approached.
Children have reacted positively to
all the media mentioned, including
associated methods of working,
such as collage and construction.
Neither the text, nor the illustrations are intended to be a complete
'how to do it manual'. They are
rather an approach towards
methods which will enable children
to carry out, simply and
inexpensively, an expansion of
their ideas.

Printmaking is often criticized
as a 'mechanical' method of expression. However, for the self-
conscious child, who may feel that
he cannot paint or draw, this very
'mechanical' feeling may prove to
be an advantage, helping to break
down the child's inhibitions and
building his self-confidence in the
communication of ideas.

Possibly the worst form of art
education that children can have is
one in which they are taught to
emulate a style or standard of
painting whatever that style or
standard may be. Children should
be encouraged to think for themselves rather than to master a
number of visual skills. In this
respect printmaking should never
be allowed to become an isolated
activity.

Working along these lines is
difficult and arduous for the
teacher, for it involves participa-
tion and understanding. It is,
however, infinitely rewarding.
'No material of any practical value
should be despised; only your
talent will define the limits of
achievement whatever materials
you use.'
Michael Rothenstein.

11

Right. Fig. 9. 'Fur Coat'.
Relief print made by inking a fur coat.
Harvey Daniels, Peter Hawes, Silvie Turner
working together. Printed on an Albion
Press.

Right. Fig. 10. 'Book of Flags'.
Girl, age 17. Potato cuts. A very simple
technique used here by an older student.

13

Left. Fig. 11. 'Mask'.
Boy, age 12. Silk-screen stencil print in two colours. (Imberhorne Comprehensive School, East Grinstead.)

Below. Fig. 12. 'Shirt'.
Child, age 12. Corrugated cardboard print. (Redbridge Art Centre.)

Below. Fig. 13. 'Pirate'.
Ivo Rousham, age 9. Stamp print made with junk collected by Ivo. (East Sussex County Art Centre, Lewes.)

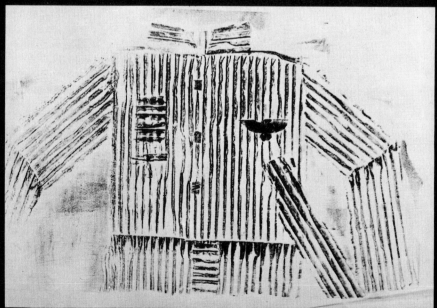

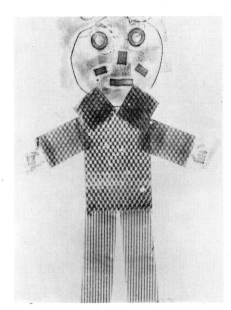

Right. Fig. 14. 'Man'.
Karen Surges, age 9. Roller rubbing in
which an inked roller or brayer was rolled
on top of the printing paper which had
metal objects arranged underneath.
(Saturday morning children's classes, Ohio
University. Instructor Melody Weiler.)

Right. Fig. 15. 'Fish'.
Sarah Hadley, age 5. This is a stencil print
made at home using black acrylic ink.

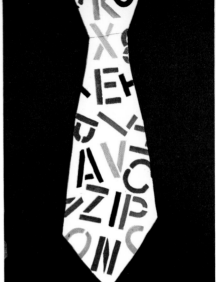

Left. Fig. 16. Bathroom tiles designed by
Oliver Williams.

Above. Fig. 17. Cut-out tie, stencilled with
coloured numbers.

Opposite top. Fig. 18. 'Titlepages'.
Foundation year, age 17-18. Cardboard
prints with type. (Bath Academy of Art.
Instructor Silvie Turner.)

Right. Fig. 19. 'La Dance au Moulin Rouge'.
Lithograph. Toulouse-Lautrec, French,
1864–1901. Courtesy of Victoria and Albert
Museum, London.

Far right. Fig. 20. Emily, age 5, used
various print methods in her 'self portrait'
including a monoprint drawing of the
spots on her dress and a stamp print of her
own arms. She then cut out the print,
which was almost life-size, because she
thought this would make it more like
herself. (East Sussex County Art Centre,
Lewes.)

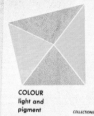

COLOUR
light and
pigment
COLLECTIONS

COLOUR
light and
pigment
COLLECTIONS

COLLECTIONS
COLOUR LIGHT AND PIGMENT

COLOUR

light and
pigment

Right. Fig. 22. 'Rocket'.
Patrick Eunis, age 14. Relief block. It
would have been difficult to find a more
direct way of producing such a strong
black and white image except with a lino
cut. (Willesden High School. Instructor
John May.)

Below. Fig. 23. 'Shoelikeness'.
Oey Tjeng Sit, Indonesian/Dutch, born 1917.
Lino cut. This is a good example of the
inherent qualities of this method of
printmaking.

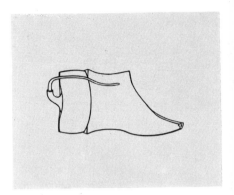

Below. Fig. 21. Child's bedroom showing
various printed surfaces.

Above. Fig. 24. Cut paper stencil used for a
'mask' print.

Right. Fig. 25. A simple everyday object printed in various ways: stencil, offset, rubbing, intaglio, relief.

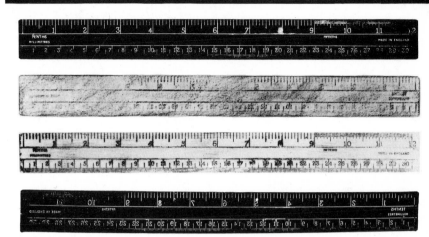

Fig. 26. 'Self Portrait'.
Carol Dove, age 7. A complex mixed media print, which held the child's interest while she solved the problems of printing parts of her body. Putting lipstick on her lips and kissing the paper was one solution. Inking her arms and printing them was another; another was the printing of her freckles. (East Sussex County Art Centre, Lewes.)

Figs. 27–30. Prints made on fabric. These can be cut up and used for dress materials, cushions or curtains. Students, age 17–18. (Newton Park College. Instructor David Andrews.)

Fig. 31. Cardboard print of a cube,
showing merges.

Chapter 1
MATERIALS
AND TOOLS

Left. Fig. 32. Equipment trolley and selection of simple tools, many of which can be found in the home.

Part of a child's learning process lies in finding out or discovering new ways of using materials to help solve a problem. The lists of various types of materials are only meant as starting points, either for investigation into the materials themselves, or as an indication for further research. The materials listed in this chapter are common to most methods but to save repetition they are included here and are referred to as the 'General List' elsewhere in the book. As you will see, many of the items listed here can easily be found around the house.

GENERAL LIST

Containers for mixing, storing, thinning, reducing, measuring: *tin cans, jars, paper cups, yoghurt containers, measuring jugs, cake tins.*

For mixing inks: *pastry and kitchen knives, spoons, any suitable kitchen utensils.*

For printing or rolling up bases: *glass slab, marble slab, plastic laminate sheet, table top, metal sheet.*

For rolling up and inking blocks: *sponge, paint, rubber or composition roller, foam rubber, padded rag, paint brush.*

For burnishing: *metal or wooden spoons, rolling pin, iron.*

For holding paper when printing: *weights from weighing scales, spanners, wrenches.*

For packing: *newspapers, old blankets, blotting paper.*

For cleaning: *turpentine/white spirit, soap, hose pipe, sink, rags, newspaper, hand cleaner, dustbin.*

Fig. 33. Corner of an artist's studio.

Fig. 34. An ordinary household mangle or wringer found in a junk yard.

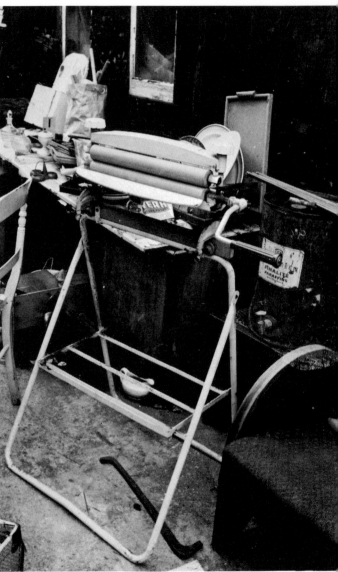

PAPER

All paper is basically made in the same way. Raw materials are mashed to a pulp and then this pulp is flattened into sheets either by hand or machine and dried.

Machine-made papers are usually made from Esparto grass, straw or wood pulp and are generally the cheaper papers. More expensive are the handmade papers made from white cotton and linen rags. Japanese paper, made from vegetable fibre, is soft, absorbent and quite expensive. It is made in many colours and often has different textures dried into the paper itself.

Sized papers, which are coated with glue or china clay so as to absorb less ink when printing, include brown paper, wrapping paper, poster paper, writing paper, shopping bags, and art (shiny) paper. Sizing also helps to stiffen the paper. Unsized papers, which are usually more absorbent to ink, softer to print on and often whiter in colour, include blotting paper, filter, newspaper, handmade and rag paper.

Examples of easily available inexpensive papers for printing include wallpaper, used envelopes, corrugated cardboard, newspapers. The type of paper should be adapted to suit your ideas.

INKS

Printing ink is made by adding colouring or pigment to a base. Pigments are obtained mainly from natural materials such as lead, minerals, earth deposits, fruit and plants.

Oil-based inks: The colour and consistency depends on the amount of pigment added to a base of linseed oil and varnish. The oil binds the pigment together.

Water-based inks: Pigment is mixed into a base of gum arabic, with the result that the inks are soluble in water. To allow the printing paper to show through a transparent base is added to the pigment. Depending on the concentration of the pigment, a colour will be either transparent or opaque, the latter completely covering most others on which it is overprinted.

Metallic inks: In a metallic ink, metal pigment is suspended in an oil base. This may be ready mixed or in a powder form to be added to a separate base. In some cases varnish or a base may be printed separately, the metallic powder being dusted onto the base immediately after printing.

Powder paint, fabric dyes, acrylic and poster colour, emulsion and other types of household paint are a few examples of other media

Fig. 35. Diagram of a simple book press and garden roller press.

Fig. 36. Hanging and stacking printing. Clothes-pegs, bulldog clips or paper clips attached to a line of string or nylon thread can be used for hanging up prints to dry. Stacking is a good method for drying prints horizontally, without danger of damage.

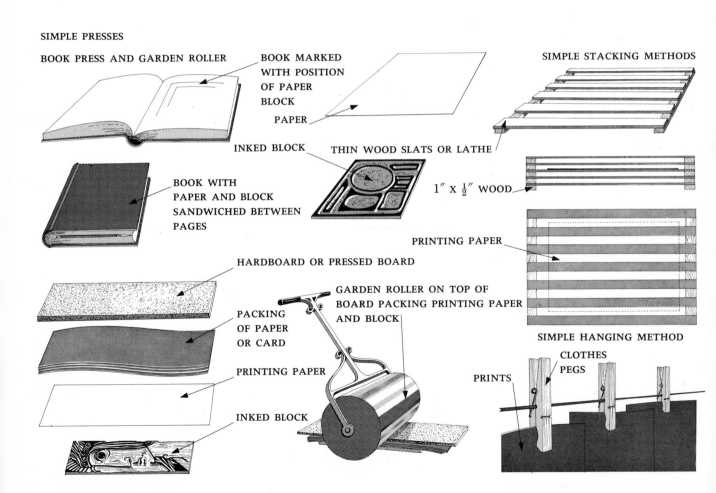

SIMPLE PRESSES

BOOK PRESS AND GARDEN ROLLER

BOOK MARKED WITH POSITION OF PAPER BLOCK

PAPER

SIMPLE STACKING METHODS

INKED BLOCK

BOOK WITH PAPER AND BLOCK SANDWICHED BETWEEN PAGES

THIN WOOD SLATS OR LATHE

$1'' \times \frac{1}{2}''$ WOOD

PRINTING PAPER

HARDBOARD OR PRESSED BOARD

PACKING OF PAPER OR CARD

PRINTING PAPER

INKED BLOCK

GARDEN ROLLER ON TOP OF BOARD PACKING PRINTING PAPER AND BLOCK

SIMPLE HANGING METHOD

CLOTHES PEGS

PRINTS

that can be used for printing.

Any form of water-based ink or paint can be added to an easily made up base, such as a wallpaper paste. This is used especially in silk-screen printing (see page 89).

Various additives to inks can be bought from specialist suppliers. These include thinners, transparent bases or reducing media for making the ink more transparent, retarders for slowing the drying of the ink, and dryers for speeding it up.

household mangle or wringer roller. For this the block and paper are placed between hardboard or cardboard and fed between two rollers by turning a handle (see Figs. 34-5).

PRESSES

Many blocks can be printed by burnishing with a wooden spoon. A press, however, may be easily made or adapted from household equipment. The simplest form of 'press' is made by placing hardboard or wood, on top of the block, paper and packing, and standing on the hardboard. Another is the

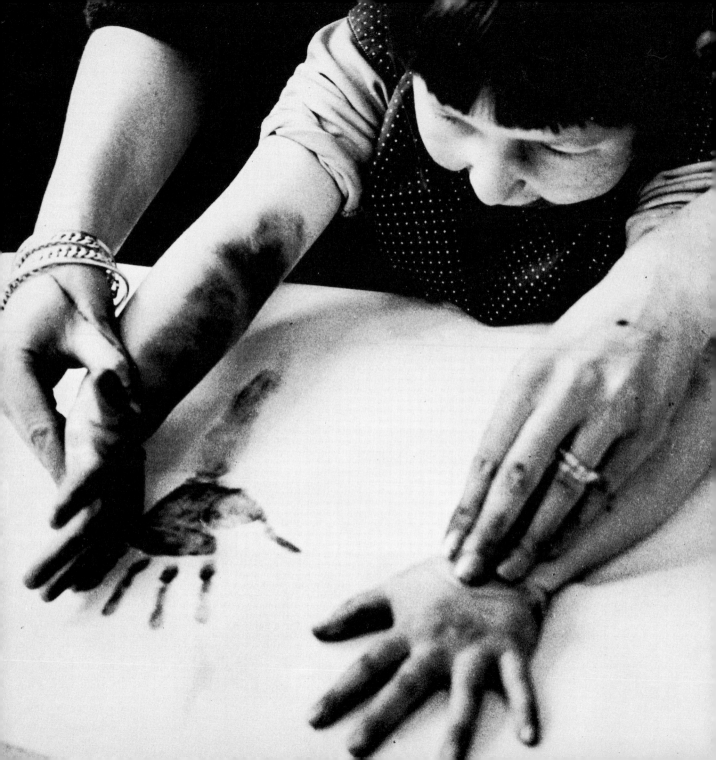

Chapter 2
STAMP PRINTING

Fig. 38. 'Anthropometrics' 1961.
Yves Klein, French, 1928–62.
Stamp prints on canvas. Here the artist
directed a group of women who applied
paint to their bodies and stamped
themselves onto canvas.
Rights reserved A.D.A.G.P., Paris 1972.

Left. Fig. 37. Emily, age 5, stamping her
arms. This shows the enjoyment children
can get from stamping parts of their body.

'It happened one day, about noon,
going towards my boat, I was
exceedingly surprised with the
print of a man's naked foot on the
shore, which was very plain to be
seen in the sand. I stood like one
thunderstruck . . . for there was
exactly the very print of a foot –
toes, heel, and every part of a foot.'
Robinson Crusoe. Daniel Defoe.

A stamp print is very simple to
make, and the amount of pre-
paration and materials needed is
minimal. Basically stamp printing
consists of inking one surface
which is then pressed (stamped)
onto another surface. This form of
printing has been used since the
Stone Age when man decorated his
cave by covering his hands with dye
and stamping them onto the cave
walls. It is still used today by
modern artists such as Yves Klein
and Steinberg, the cartoonist.

Stamp printing has many
advantages, particularly for very
young children. As Daniel Defoe's
narrative suggests, there is some-
thing magical in an unspoilt
surface. Children delight in making
footprints in clean sand or new
snow. In the same way, young
children enjoy the banging or
stamping of an object onto a blank
sheet of paper and discovering a
specific mark as the result of their
handiwork.

There are few simpler forms of
printmaking than making a potato
print. This simple method can
produce images as powerful as the
potato animals by Jonathan Kail,
age 6 (see Fig. 41). Very young
children can master this method of
printing easily, and are given a
sense of achievement because the
results are so immediate. Another
advantage of stamp printing is the
ease with which the image can be
repeated (see Fig. 50). Also
many different objects can be

29

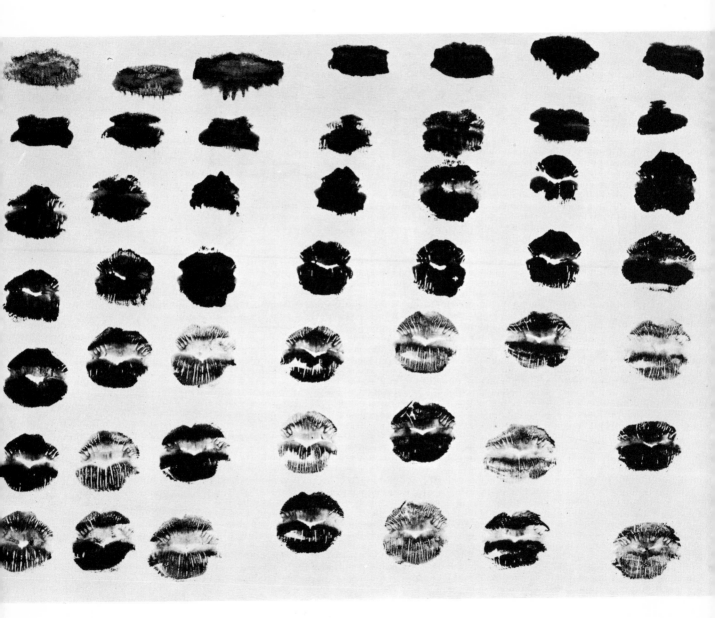

Left. Fig. 39. 'Lips'.
Girl, age 14. This repeat stamp print was obviously fun to make, completely involving the child. (Instructor Barbara Phillips.)

Below. Fig. 40. 'House'.
Boy, age 4. A stamp print, using ink pad and rubber stamp, made by a child who became fascinated with the method and produced dozens of prints.

Left. Fig. 41. 'Potato Animals' (Detail).
Jonathan Kail, age 6. Stamp print.

stamped together on the same sheet.

The printed images from different objects vary. A print from lips will resemble the lips themselves whereas one from a soft polish pad may leave an impression of a carefully graduated tone (see Figs. 39 and 43).

Once an object is printed, it could be the starting point for research into a related idea. A simple stamp print of a pound sign instigated an idea for Fig. 42, 'The Rise and Fall of a Pound'.

This is how the child who made the print described his idea: 'It all starts in the bottom right-hand corner with the pound and a key hole on its side, this means the door. You open the door by placing the pound (the key) in and you start to rise in the form of a railway line. On the rail the pound starts off green which means inexperience with money. After this,

people start complaining (opposing colours) and it goes down in the red. The Zs by the side mean the pound is resting or sleeping. Then the pound moves slowly upwards in conservative blue. The large sideways 'Three' is a firm footing I tried to make. It is meant to look three-dimensional and more solid but it did not work. The pound is now up in lights but all our money goes in paying off the loans. Then it goes a bit tottering and a bit green as to what's up and down they go again (they decided they were no good and put them in a bucket). The reason some prints turned out better and not for anything is because I got most of the colours from other people. Beneath the bucket the roller marks are supposed to mean the ground, this brings the whole composition down to earth.'

Other children in the classroom at the same time were making

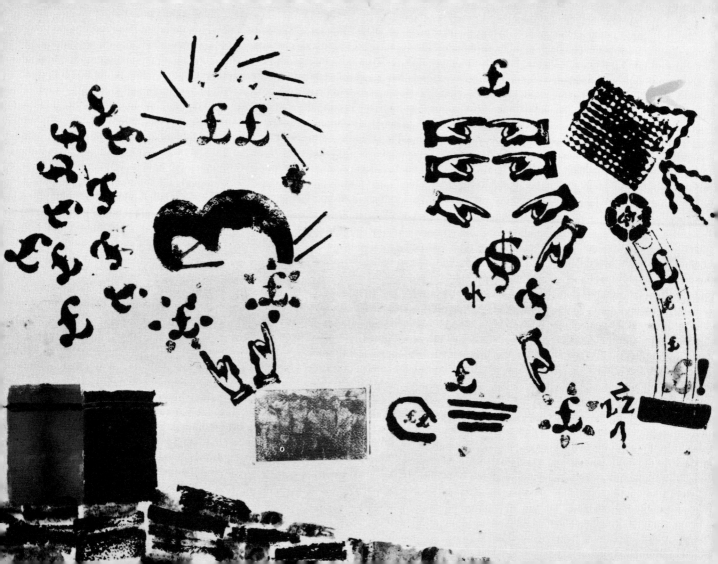

Left. Fig. 42. 'The Rise and Fall of a Pound'.
Child, age 13. Stamp print. (Imberhorne
Comprehensive School, East Grinstead.)

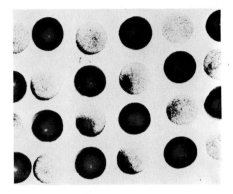

Left. Fig. 43. 'Polish Pad Print'.
Girl, age 13. (Instructor Barbara Phillips.)

games, models and other three-dimensional prints. All of the ideas for these had started from a single object stamped onto paper.

MATERIALS AND TOOLS

'General List' page 23

Ink pad, a brush for inking, sponge soaked with ink, ink on slab, post-office pad soaked with dye, water-colour paints.

Any object that can be held easily and has a reasonably flat printing surface, such as the list of materials which the head of a nursery school has used for printing with pre-school children:

Leaves, real and plastic; rubbings with crayon over scallop shells, embossed wallpaper, date stamps, different sized tubes and lids, beer bottle tops, carpeting, shaped wood, corks, linoleum, fur fabric, webbing, hair rollers, sticks, different shaped pieces of dried sponge, large sponge, photographic rollers, cotton reels/spools, pram wheels, paint and pastry wheels, corrugated cardboard rolled into cylinders of different circumferences and shapes, doilies, sink mats, undulating sheet plastic, pleated plastic lampshade, tooth-picks on blocks, heels and soles, articles of clothing, pipe cleaners on blocks, pastry cutters, feet, hands, fingers, arms, string on blocks, pot scourers, vegetables: potatoes, sliced cabbage, parsnips; combs, plugs from washbasins, rubber thimbles, all kinds of plastic waste material, grass or palm leaves, sponge dish-washing mops, rubber stamps, candles, construction bricks, wooden letter forms.

INKING THE BLOCK

If you are using a large block for stamp printing first roll out the ink on a slab with a roller and then roll the ink onto the block itself. Make sure that the ink is tacky and not runny on the roller. If you are using a small block this can be pressed directly onto an inked pad or slab or the surface can be painted directly with a brush.

The smoother the surface of your block (stamp) the thinner the film of ink should be; if you are using a block with a rough surface you will need a much thicker film of ink.

PRINTING THE BLOCK

Any smooth, stable surface can be used as a base for printing. Press or stamp the inked block directly onto the paper by hand: the amount of ink that is transferred will depend on the amount of ink on the block and the hand pressure. Inking should be repeated after each printing: with a single inking and repeated printing the image gets fainter. To pick up more detail from an uneven surface or hard block, for example scissors,

put some soft packing such as newspaper under the printing paper. It is not always necessary to use ink or paint. Lipstick is being used in Fig. 1 and a professional stamp kit has been used in Fig. 40. Another idea is to press your block into a soft surface such as clay or plasticine.

Left. Fig. 44. Still life and prints of various stamping materials. Prints from any of these materials could lead to research into a related idea.

Above. Fig. 45. 'Repeat Potato Print'. John Morgan, age 14. (Imberhorne Comprehensive School, East Grinstead. Instructor Doug Coupe.)

Right. Fig. 46. 'Feet'. Boy, age 16. Relief print.

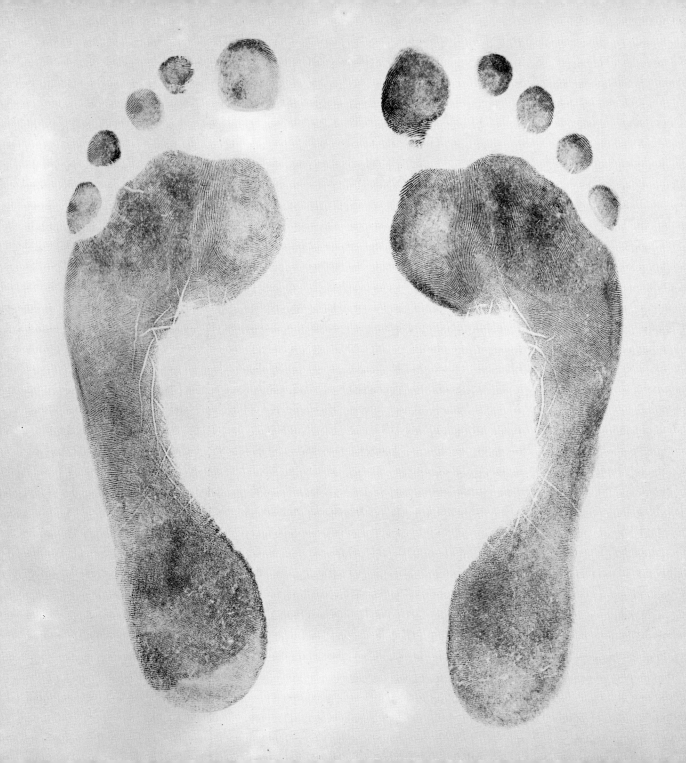

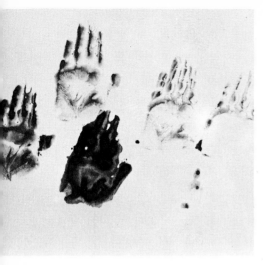

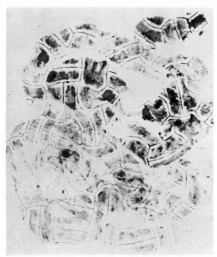

Top left. Fig. 47. 'Handstamps'.
Child, age 4. This stamp print shows the characteristic spattered image of the method.

Top right. Fig. 48. A stamp print made by painting a ball and bouncing it on paper.

Left. Fig. 49. 'Nine on Sunday'.
Helen Kail, age 9. Stamp print and rubbing.

36

Above. Fig. 50. 'Animals'.
Child, age 12. Stamp repeat of lino block,
turning one animal into a herd.
(Redbridge Art Centre.)

Left. Fig. 51. Print from a tyre tread made by driving a car over a piece of paper.

Left. 53. Emily cutting out her self portrait.

Above. Fig. 54. Stamp print being made of a pirate, using found objects.

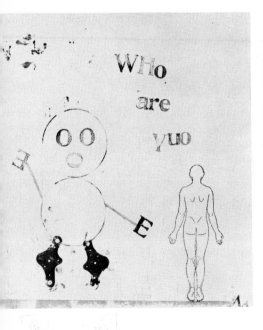

Above. Fig. 52. 'Who Are You?'. Child, age 9. Rubber stamp and wood type print.

Right. Fig. 55. 'Woollen Gloves'. Child, age 15. Relief print of a found object. Notice the amount of detail compared with Fig. 76, which is the expression of an idea. (Redbridge Art Centre.)

Fig. 56. 'My Cat's Name is Puckle'.
Ivo Rousham stamps his concrete poem,
using wooden type. This is an excellent
example of making an animal with words.

40

Figs. 57–9. Consecutive stages in making a potato print. Carol, age 7.

Chapter 3
BLOCKMAKING

Left. Fig. 60. A cardboard block of tractor made by a child, age 9. (Redbridge Art Centre.)

In this chapter blockmaking is defined as a collection of materials which are assembled together and attached to a base. This particular method is not a subtractive method in which parts of the surface block are taken away, it is additive.

When different objects are assembled and stuck together on a block, the meaning of each individual object alters because of its relationship with the other material on the block. This can often be exciting and revealing to the child when the block is printed and the discipline involved in the collection and assembly of objects may help children who are unsure of their own creative ability.

The processes involved in this type of blockmaking are closely allied to collage, which is the pasting of paper and other materials onto a surface. Both hard and soft materials can be used and objects need not necessarily be of the same height, though some degree of uniformity is advisable (see Fig. 61). The children themselves will discover and collect most of the materials needed and as they collect, assemble and print them they will develop a fresh awareness of familiar objects which are brought into sharper focus.

Children should be encouraged to experiment and express their ideas in the creative use of the block and they should avoid thinking narrowly along any particular path that is considered safe. A block need not necessarily be printed but may be seen as a three-dimensional piece of work in itself.

MATERIALS AND TOOLS
General List page 23

Collograph or Collaged Block
materials for the block, for example, string, peas, clips;

Below. Fig. 62. A glue block made by pulling a comb through the glue.

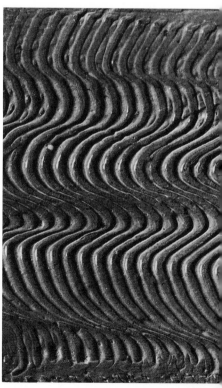

44

glue such as Evostick, Elmers or any slow drying glue;
glue spreader, brush, or piece of cardboard;
base for block such as thin cardboard, hardboard, masonite or wood. The following is a list of readily available objects that can be easily printed and which are not often used: *dustbin lid, rubber mat, toys, clothes, paper clips, jewellery.*

Cardboard Block
Blocks may be made up entirely from cut out cardboard shapes (see Fig. 60). Pieces of corrugated cardboard can also be cut up and stuck to a base.

Glue Block
base (see above);
unibond or Bostic, or any thick glue;
implements for drawing or pressing into glue, for example, a cardboard tube or carton.

Plaster Block
wooden frame or tray or box;
plaster of paris, water and mixing can or bowl;
grease – lard or vaseline;
objects to press into plaster.

HOW TO MAKE THE BLOCK

Collograph and Cardboard Block
Spread glue over the base and then stick objects down firmly. The glue should preferably be slow drying as this permits work on the block over a period of time and rearrangement of the objects on the block. Alternatively it can be thickly spread or more glue applied if it dries.

Objects that are stuck down onto the block should be of a reasonably uniform height as only the top surface of the collograph prints. When all the objects have been placed in position leave weights on top of the block to

Right. Fig. 64. 'Railway Journey'.
A section of a panoramic print made very
quickly by stamping.

Right. Fig. 68. 'Garderobe' 1947.
Rolf Nesch, Norwegian, born 1893.
Found object intaglio print, which contains
pieces of wire, netting and found metal
objects. Notice how they lose their identity
and become elements in a whole.
(Courtesy Victoria and Albert Museum.)

Above. Fig. 65. 'Utilabrake'.
Tom, age 5. Various parts of cars were
rubbed in different colours and the images
joined together on the same page.
(East Sussex County Art Centre, Lewes.)

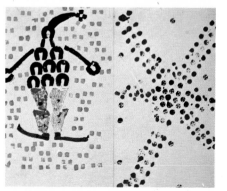

Above. Fig. 66. 'Horse'.
Inbal, age 12. Colour monoprint drawing
showing how colours can be drawn simply
and quickly in a linear way. This is one of
the great advantages of the transfer
drawing technique.

Left. Fig. 67. 'Clown' and 'Press Studs'.
L. Stockman and A. Dindolia, age 11.
Stamp prints, with the pattern built up by
the repeated stamping of very small objects.
(Willesden High School. Instructor John
May.)

46

Below. Fig. 69. 'Mural'.
Children, age 7-11. A combined print, made
by rubbing of string blocks. Several blocks
have been printed together to form a mural.
(Saturday morning children's classes, Ohio
University. Instructor Melody Weiler.)

Below. Fig. 70. 'Bobby, age 8'.
Roller rubbing on string block and relief
print. (Saturday morning children's classes,
Ohio University. Instructor Melody Weiler.)

Below. Fig. 71. String block of 'Elephant' by Greta, age 5. Making this block is a completely different but related activity to painting and drawing.

Right. Fig. 72. This plaster block with an imprint of lace emphasizes the delicacy and detail of the original material. (Redbridge Art Centre.)

Above. Fig. 73.
Patrick making embossed glue block of circles with toilet toll.

Right. Fig. 74.
Children making blocks from a collection of materials. (East Sussex County Art Centre, Lewes.)

Right. Fig. 75. 'Space Car'.
Child, age 12. Here printed blocks and
stamped objects are combined.

Below. Fig. 76. 'Handshake'.
Ben Anthony, age 10. Relief print and
polystyrene (styrofoam) block, illustrating
an idea and not merely a technical exercise.
Printing the gloves enabled Ben to convey
his idea directly. (East Sussex County
Art Centre, Lewes.)

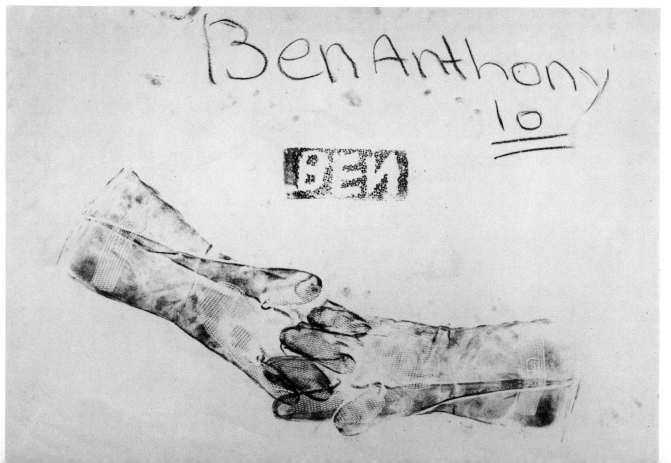

Below. Fig. 77. Girl inking up a corrugated cardboard block with a roller.

Left. Fig. 78. Patrick, age 5, holding his block of a 'Mechanical Man', made from paper clips, screws, peas and junk, stuck with glue on to strawboard.

Below. Fig. 79. 'Aeroplane'. L. Knight, age 12. Corrugated cardboard print.

Right. **Fig. 80.** 'Numbers'. Corrugated cardboard print, made by remedial children age 12-13. A number has been created by cutting the corrugated cardboard to change the direction of the line. (St. George's School, Bristol. Instructor Judy Brooks).

hold objects firmly in place while the glue is drying. Leave the block until it is thoroughly dry.

Glue Block
Pour a layer of glue over the base roughly 1/8 inch deep, and leave it until it becomes tacky. When it is tacky press a variety of objects on the surface so that they leave marks; for example, a comb may be pulled through the glue to leave tracks (see Fig. 62).

Plaster Block
Always add the plaster to the water when mixing and not vice-versa. Sprinkle sufficient plaster into the water until it comes up to the surface of the water. The water is then said to be saturated with plaster.

When the plaster is mixed it should have a creamy consistency.

Rub the objects with grease to stop them sticking to the plaster when it dries and lightly grease the tray or box as well. Place objects on the tray, making sure that the walls are higher than the object and pour the plaster into the centre of the tray. Pour the plaster in slowly as this avoids air bubbles. When the plaster is set, remove the block from the tray and take out the objects. The block needs two days to dry out completely.

INKING THE BLOCK
To facilitate printing, seal the surface of the block with ink by rolling it up, and allow it to dry. This will also give an indication of the printed image. Then roll out a layer of ink on a slab using a hard roller. Thoroughly ink the surface of the block. A hard roller and light pressure inks the top surface of the block. A soft roller and increased pressure inks deeper.

PRINTING THE BLOCK
Making a block and printing it should be done in separate parts of a room to avoid mess, congestion and dirty printing. Lay the paper on top of the inked block. The print is taken by applying pressure onto the upper side of the printing paper. For this a rubber roller, wooden spoon or sponge may be used. When burnishing with a spoon hold the handle of the spoon with one hand and press the fingers of the other hand onto the back of the spoon.

Right. Fig. 84. 'Monoprint Drawing'. Michael. (Saturday morning children's classes, Ohio University. Instructor Melody Weiler.)

Above. Fig. 82. 'Elephants'. Greta, age 5. Rubbing of a string block. (Putenham College of Education, Laboratory School, Ohio. Instructor Harvey Daniels.)

Fig. 83. 'Mark, age 8'. String block and relief print. (Saturday morning children's classes, Ohio University. Instructor Melody Weiler.)

Name Michael

Chapter 4
SIMPLE TRANSFER PRINTING

Left. Fig. 85. 'Charlie Brown'. Transfer drawing. (Saturday morning children's classes, Ohio University. Instructor Melody Weiler.)

There are various methods of transfer printing and all of them in this chapter are extremely simple to do and generally 'one-off' impressions. The emphasis is on the transference of the image onto the paper and the print is usually taken by hand pressure. The freedom and the directness of most of the techniques discussed in this chapter make them useful as an introduction to printmaking.

Monoprinting, that is drawing or painting on a base and then taking a print from the base, allows the child who enjoys working with paint, the freedom to make his own marks while retaining the logic of the print (see Fig. 88). The particular organic quality of the ink apparent in this method is unobtainable by any other means. For instance, when the ink runs on the base or if two pieces of paper are sandwiched together and then pulled apart, the transference of the design is subtle and varied, and no painting could achieve the same result. Many colours can also be used together and printed at the same time.

This form of printmaking is closer to drawing and painting than any of the print methods mentioned in previous chapters, as a block is generally not used, and ink or paint is often applied directly with a brush before printing takes place.

Transfer drawing also has a very distinctive character (see Fig. 87). It is the only method by which many colours can be drawn in a linear way, simply and quickly, producing an unexpected and exciting quality (see Fig. 66). With the method of the transfer print (see Fig. 90) an image from an actual magazine photograph can be made and the child can use his own magazines or comics for material.

Rubbings can be taken from

Right. Fig. 88. 'Uder Worter'.
Jason, age 8. Underwater animals, using
monoprinting methods. The marks are
made freely yet the finished work retains
the logic of the print. (East Sussex County
Art Centre, Lewes.)

Fig. 87. 'Le Mans 180 Racing Car'.
C. Davies and I. Helman. An excellent
example of the distinctive character of
transfer drawing. (Saturday morning
children's classes, Ohio University.
Instructor Melody Weiler.)

anything with a slightly relief
surface, the results often intensify-
ing certain aspects of the object.
Three-dimensional objects can be
rubbed by bending paper around
them (see Fig. 91).

In contrast to other transfer
methods, a roller offset leaves clear,
detailed and sharp images from a particular object or surface (see Fig. 89).

In most of the transfer methods
there is a very strong element of
chance which can be controlled
only to a certain degree. This holds
exciting possibilities for the
imaginative user (see Fig. 92).

As an example of how these
methods can be used, Melody
Weiler writes about the Saturday
morning activity in a workshop at
Ohio University:
'I purchased several large boxes
from a moving company. Upon
hearing of the project the company
donated the materials. The kids
decided to make a farm. They

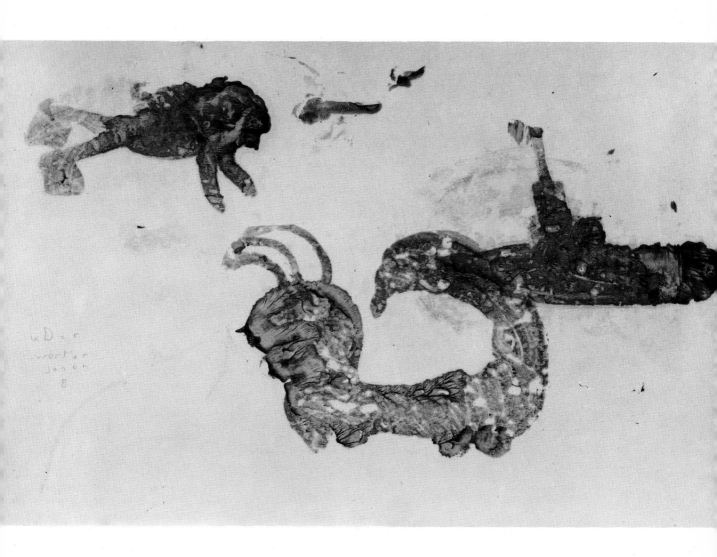

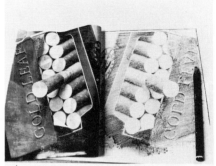

Above left. Fig. 89. A roller offset print of a pair of scissors.

Above. Fig. 90. Transfer print of a colour photograph from a magazine. Notice the rubbing marks of the soft pencil.

Left. Fig. 91. Child wearing a rubbing made from his own plimsolls. Paper was wrapped round the plimsolls to make the rubbing.

Right. Fig. 92. 'Monoprint'.
Maurice Prendergast, American, 1859–1924.
This monoprint illustrates that the chance elements inherent in this method may be controlled with experience.
(Courtesy of the Brooklyn Museum.)

61

Below. Fig. 95. Monoprint being lifted from ink slab by Carol, age 7.

Below. Fig. 96. Examples of transfer rubbings taken from magazines.

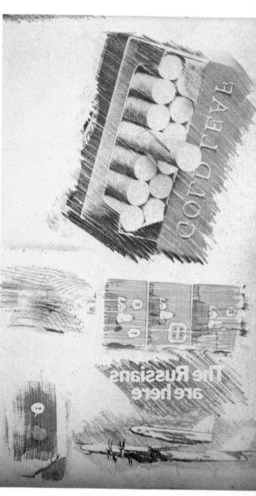

Left. Fig. 97. 'Decalcomania'. Conroy Maddox, British, born 1920. (Courtesy H. D. and J. Daniels.)

Figs. 98–9. Two stages in making transfer drawing by Patrick, age 5.

Below. Fig. 100. A print of scissors taken from the inked-up roller.

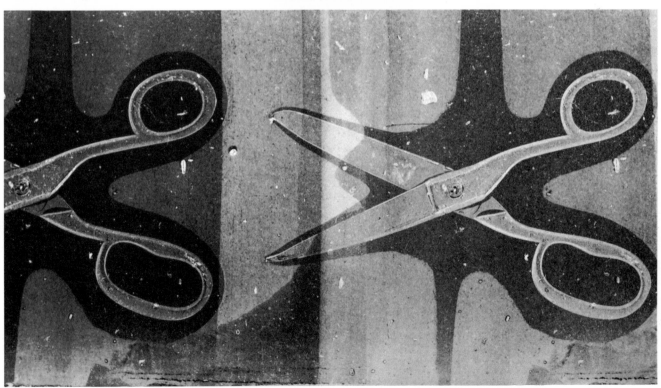

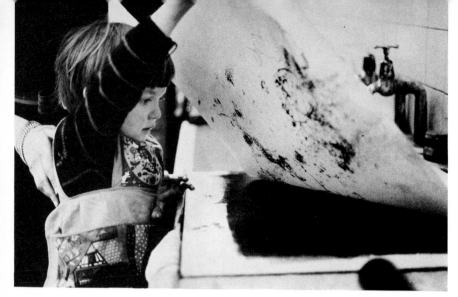

made a farm house, a barn, a garage and some animals. Rubbings were taken from the walls of the room, getting such textures as brick, metal and wood. These textures were then cut out and pasted with rubber cement to conform to the buildings. Working on a 2-D surface and then transferring this into the 3-D was quite an undertaking. Margaret and Gizele made curtains for their room. Their front door also had a realistic-looking paper doorknob. Bobby Betz made the chimney for the house with smoke to give it the impression that some people lived there. It was this project that led us into our first play. Bobby Betz brought in the record of 'Dragnet' and an opera was sung by Spike Jones and his gang. With only one week to go before the big production the kids made all their costumes and practised their lines, which were all mimed. The farm

they had been working on during the work shop became their stage set.'

This shows how an activity that starts as a printmaking exercise can develop. This type of activity can be of great benefit to the child.

MATERIALS AND TOOLS
General list page 23
Transfer Drawing: *pencil or hard sharp-pointed tool, ink slab, ink (oil-based)*

Transfer Printing: *magazine photographs, turpentine, white spirit, paint remover, methylated spirit, large soft pencil or handle of wooden spoon.*

Monoprinting: *ink slab, e.g. glass formica, acetate, oil-based inks or water paints, turpentine, white spirits or water brushes.*

Rubbing: *cobbler's wax, grease crayon, soft pencil, or lithographic chalk, thin, strong paper.*

Roller Offset: *oil-based inks, soft gelatine roller, hard inking roller, rag.*

Marbling: *sink or large bowl, water, oil-based inks, turpentine or white spirit, absorbent paper.*

Decalcomania: *paper, any ink, water-based paints or India drawing ink.*

METHODS OF PRINTING
Transfer Drawing
Roll out a very thin, even distribution of ink onto a smooth dust-free surface, for example, a glass slab or litho stone. The texture of the ink should be dry and tacky, not wet. Lower the printing paper gently onto the ink.

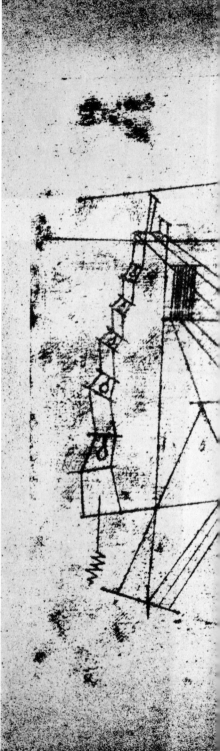

Above. Fig. 101. Roller offset being taken of a pair of scissors.

Right. Fig. 102. 'Tightrope Walker'. Paul Klee, Swiss/German, 1879–1940. Transfer drawing. (© by S.P.A.D.E.M., Paris 1971. Courtesy of Bibliothèque Nationale, Paris.)

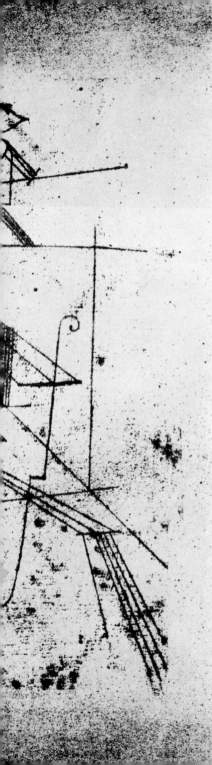

Make a drawing on the back of the paper with a ballpoint pen, knitting needle, piece of wood, finger, or any sharp object. The paper will pick up ink only where pressure has been exerted (see Fig. 85).

Transfer Printing
Cut out photographs either in colour or black and white from magazines.

Soak the photographs on the back with turps or white spirit and leave them for three minutes.

Place the required image face downwards onto the printing paper and hold it there firmly.

Rub the entire surface evenly with a soft pencil or bone folder (see Fig. 96).
Note: Different magazines react to different solvents.

Monoprinting
Make the design on a glass slab or litho stone using thinned oil paint. More than one colour can be painted on the slab at the same time. Place the design under the glass (if you are using one) as a guide. Lower the paper onto the glass.

A print from the ink is transferred to the paper by pressure of the hand or roller on the back of the paper. When colour is required in a specific place it can be added in successive printings, if the print is replaced in the same position on the glass (see Fig. 95).

Rubbing
Place the paper over the surface to be rubbed and hold it firmly in position with weights or tape. Work over the whole surface evenly with a crayon. The crayon will be more effectively used if held flat (see Fig. 93).

Roller Offset
Roll a thin, even layer of ink onto

Fig. 103. 'A Shake Game'.
Inigo, age 7. A relief stamp and rubbing.

Fig. 104. Marbling print being lifted out of water.

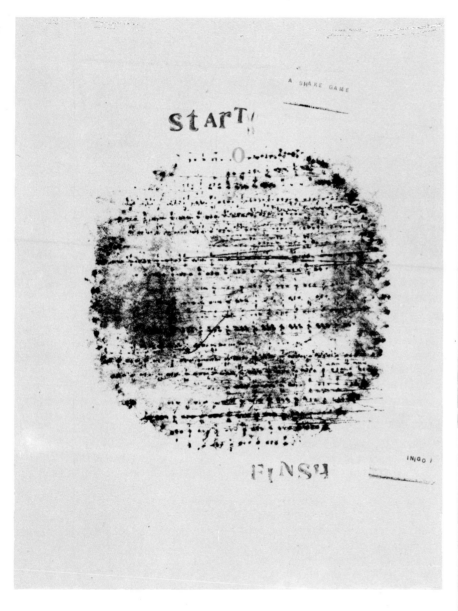

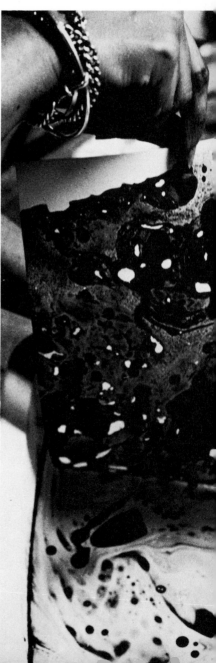

Fig. 105. 'Giraffes'.
Marie, age 7. Rubbing of string block.
(Putenham College of Education, Laboratory
School, Ohio. Instructor Harvey Daniels.)

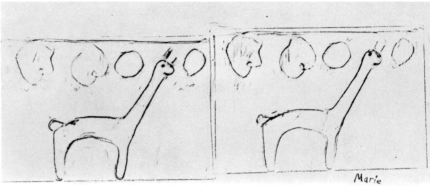

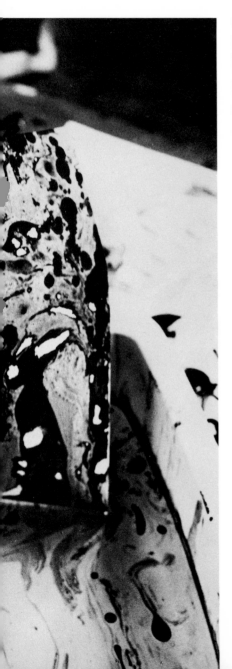

the object or surface to be printed.

Pass a clear, soft gelatine roller evenly and slowly over the inked object or surface.

Pass the roller slowly and firmly over a clean piece of paper and the image will then be transferred from the gelatine roller onto the printing paper (see Fig. 89).

Marbling

Half fill a sink, pan or bowl with water. Thin down oil paint or printing ink and pour it onto the surface of the water. Stir the water and oil paint, for example with a comb or wooden spoon. Lay the paper on the surface of the water. When the paper is lifted the top surface of both oil and water will transfer onto the paper (see Fig. 104). Dry the paper by stretching it on a board with drawing pins or tape

Decalcomania

Paint or draw with ink onto one half of a sheet of paper. Fold the paper in half and press it together. When the paper is opened the image formed will be identical on either side (see Fig. 97).

Chapter 5
CUTTING

Cutting involves the gouging, engraving or carving away of a surface. The cut-away parts, being lower, remain white when the block is inked and printed. Carving and engraving are traditional methods of making blocks and the use of cutting tools is closely allied to a traditional craftsman's approach.

The method is not as simple as those previously discussed; it requires greater physical control and muscular effort as the material of the block is often tough and resistant. However, children not only often enjoy gouging lino or wood, but in addition they also enjoy the effort of working with and looking after the cutting tools.

Wood or linoleum cutting are very suitable methods for children who like to work slowly and methodically as work on the block can take a long time to perfect (see Figs. 106 and 107).

Most of the materials mentioned in this chapter can also be used as cut-out flat colour shapes for printing (see Fig. 108). Nevertheless, each material when cut and printed has its own particular characteristics (see Figs. 110 and 112).

Block cutting is a suitable medium for printing illustrations and for posters, as large numbers of copies can be taken from a single block, which is often of a more durable nature than blocks used in simpler printing. The blocks can be stored for a long time and then re-used.

MATERIALS AND TOOLS

In this chapter blocks can be divided into two kinds, those with a pronounced surface character, for example, wood, and those with a smooth surface, for example, linoleum.

Fig. 107. 'Three Birds'.
Children, age 13. Black lino cuts made by
cutting away large areas of the lino and
leaving only the lines to be printed.
(Willesden High School. Instructor John May.)

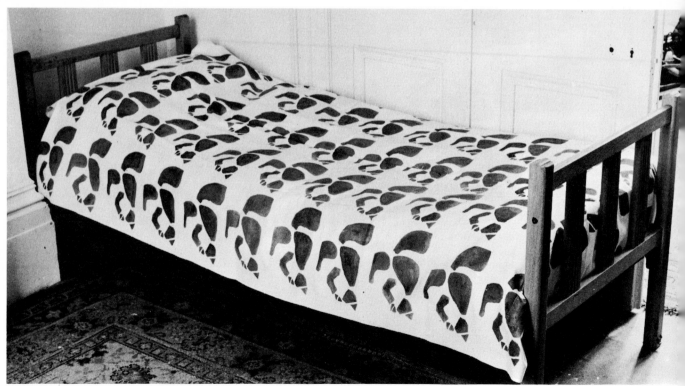

Figs. 109–10. 'Micky Mouse' and 'Goofy'. Geoffrey Stewart, age 12. White line lino cuts illustrating the sharp and precise lines made by cutting into a lino block. (Saturday morning children's classes, Ohio University. Instructor Melody Weiler.)

 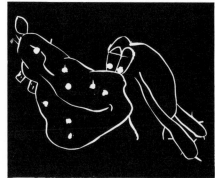

Left. Fig. 108. 'Bedcover'. Child, age 13. Repeat of squirrel lino block printed on fabric. (Mary Sheafe School, Cranbrook, Kent. Instructor Mrs. V. Reynolds.)

Pronounced Surface

Wood: hard or soft. The grain can be rubbed up with a stiff wire brush. This increases the effect of the grain. It should be free of knots, and planed if necessary.

Hard woods: *hornbeam, cedar, sycamore, maple, teak.*
Soft woods: *pear, box, apple, soft pine, redpine.*

Plywood: the surface can be rubbed up easily. Too thin a gauge bends badly with use.

Hardboard: inexpensive and has a hard surface. It can be scratched with sandpaper, needles, or nails.

Polystyrene: soft surfaced. Tiles or blocks can be cut or shaped with a Stanley (exacto) knife or a heated wire cutter. The top surface can be scraped away.

Smooth Surface

Linoleum: any plain colour. New lino is easy to cut because it is softer than old lino, which should be heated gently before cutting.

Sheet rubber: flexible, easily cut and marked.

Plastic: tough, hard material, slippery to handle, needs heating gently before use although care must be taken that there is adequate ventilation when doing this. Good surface for handpower tools to be used on.

Tools: *'V'-shaped tools, wood carving tools, engraving tools, hard roller or brayer, wooden spoon, burin, stamps, mallet, weights, jig, plastic wood, first aid box.*

74

Left. Fig. 111. 'The Last Hour', 1920. Edvard Munch, Norwegian, 1863–1944. Woodcut. The artist has used the grain of the plankwood to enhance his expressionistic ideas. (Courtesy Graphische Sammlung Albertina, Vienna.)

Right. Fig. 112. 'House'. Luther Roberts, British, born 1923. The characteristic lines of wood engraving used with great effect.

HOW TO MAKE BLOCKS

All of the materials mentioned in this chapter can be cut with simple tools. The method of cutting is determined by the result required and an understanding of the tools and materials. Generally a stronger tool, such as a wood carving tool, is better than the 'pen' lino cutting tool which often breaks and easily blunts. Specialized tools, such as a gauge, 'v' tools, 'u' tools, and Japanese tools are used for cutting.

If necessary, drawings can be made on to the blocks before cutting begins. India ink, if used, remains throughout the proofing stage.

The teacher should explain necessary safety requirements involving the use of sharp tools. Keep the block still when cutting by holding it with one hand, or by clamping it to a bench. A jig or bench hook is useful when cutting small blocks (see Fig. 106). It is very important to insist that children keep their hands behind the tool when cutting (see Fig. 124).

Take care not to undercut a line made in the block, otherwise the sharp edge will collapse under pressure when printed. At any time during cutting it may be useful to roll up the block with ink and take a 'proof' print. The block can then be cleaned off with white spirit and cutting continued.

When cutting small wood engravings, direct the tool with the thumb. When cutting curved lines it is usual to have a sand-filled leather bag under the block so that the block can be turned rather than the tool.

Keep all tools very sharp, especially for wood engraving (see Fig. 112).

METHODS OF PRINTING

Roll the ink out smoothly on a slab. Before inking, make sure the block is free of dust and dirt.

Left. Fig. 113. Cutting tools, roller and other equipment.

Right. Fig. 114. 'Bees coming out of a Hive'. This is an old engraving used by a printer for a book illustration. The block itself has been printed many hundreds of times.

Ink the top surface of the block evenly with a roller or brayer.

Place paper on top of the inked block and, if necessary, hold it in position by weights.

Burnish the surface of the block evenly with a wooden spoon or clean hard roller.

At intervals lift the print carefully to see how the printing is progressing.

ELIMINATION METHOD
The elimination method is a simple way of producing colour prints. A number of copies are made in the printing of the first colour. The block is then cleaned and more lino is cut away. The recut block is then reprinted on top of the first colour in exactly the same position, but in a different colour. Allow each colour to dry between printings.

This process can be repeated until there is no lino left to be cut away.

More complicated methods of colour registration and printing are discussed in the second volume.

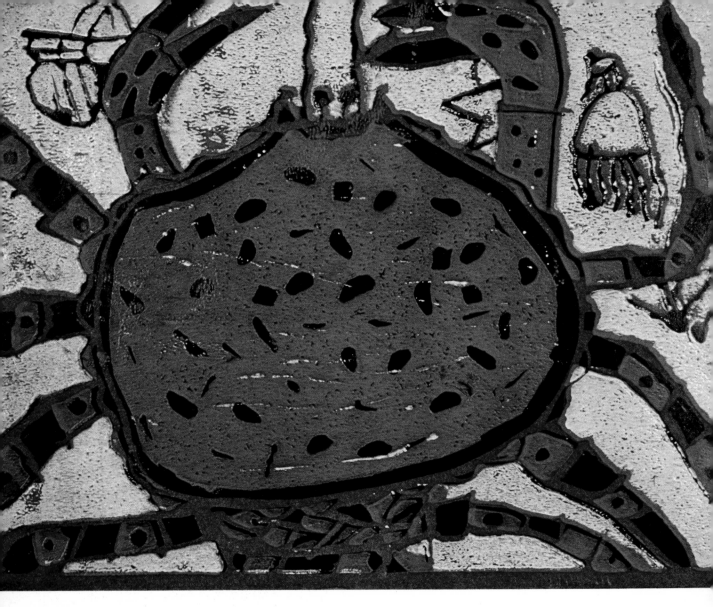

Above and *far right bottom*. Fig. 115 and Fig. 119. 'Elephant and Crab'.
Children, age 13–14. Lino cuts in colour made by the simple elimination method. (Mary Sheafe School, Cranbrook, Kent. Instructor Mrs. V. Reynolds.)

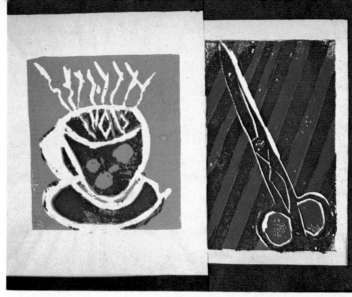

Top left. Fig. 116. 'Flower Hunting Scene'. Shiko Munakata. Woodcut printed in black and dark grey. (Collection, The Museum of Modern Art, New York.)

Bottom left. Fig. 117. 'Deux Femmes'. Pablo Picasso, Spanish, born 1881. Woodcut. (© by S.P.A.D.E.M., Paris, 1971. Courtesy Bibliothèque Nationale, Paris.)

Top right. Fig. 118. 'Scissors' and 'Tea Cup'. Children, age 12. Lino cuts of everyday objects using double-sided lino. (Highfield School, Hemel Hempstead. Instructor Judy Reid.)

79

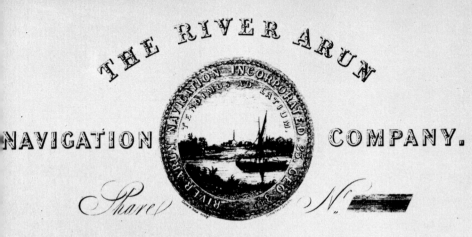

THE RIVER ARUN

NAVIGATION COMPANY.

RIVER ARUN NAVIGATION INCORPORATED 25 GEO. 3
TENDIMUS AD LATIUM.

Share   *N.°*

This is to Certify *that*

is a Proprietor of **ONE SHARE** *in the*
River Arun Navigation, *numbered as above, and*
Registered in the Register Book of the Company,
(subject to the Rules, Orders and Regulations of the said
Company) and that he, his Executors, Administrators and
Assigns are entitled to the Profits and Advantages thereof.
Dated this   day of   1842.

MIDHURST
Clerk to the Company.

Fig. 121. Children cutting lino blocks in a classroom. (Saturday morning children's classes, Ohio University. Instructor Hugh Kepets.)

Fig. 120. Copper engraving of an old share certificate.

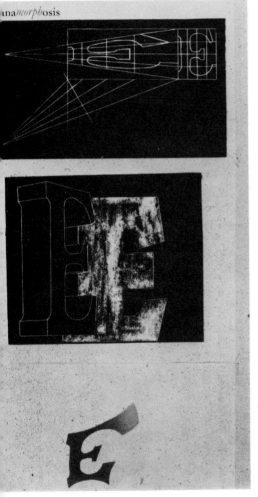

Right. Fig. 124. A lino block being cut.
Note how the hands are positioned behind
the cutting tool.

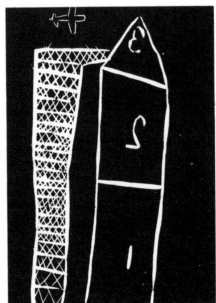

Above. Fig. 123. '3 Stages of a Rocket'.
Mary Malcolm, age 7. White line lino cuts.
The image of the rocket was cut directly
into the block leaving large areas to be
inked up and printed. (Saturday morning
children's classes, Ohio University.
Instructor Melody Weiler.)

Above. Fig. 125. 'Rabbits'.
Jennifer Boyce, age 8. A lino cut. This very
positive work was made by someone with
no obvious talent for drawing. (Saturday
morning children's classes, Ohio University.
Instructor Melody Weiler.)

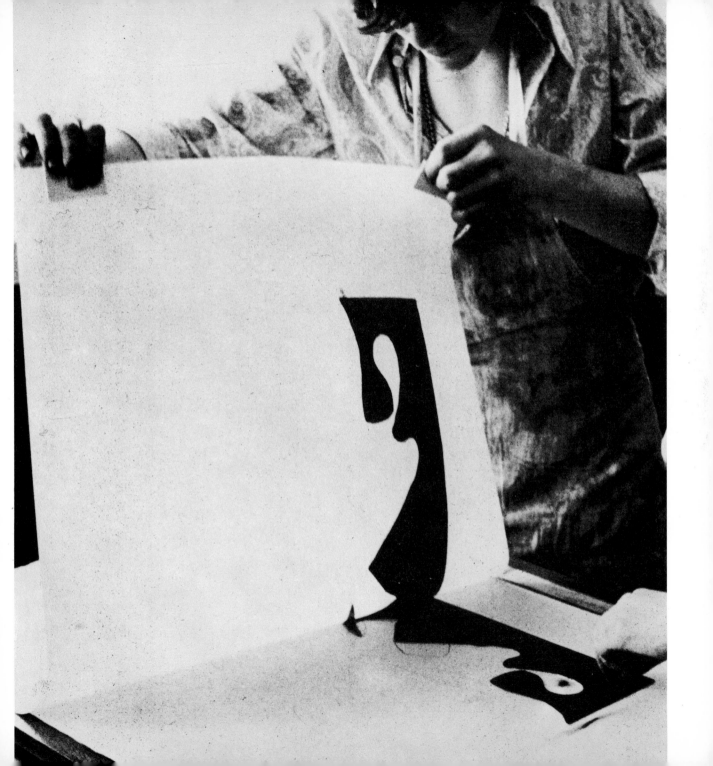

Chapter 6
STENCIL PRINTING

A brush or inked roller forces ink onto the printing paper through holes which have been made into a stencil paper. Pre-cut wax paper stencils can easily be bought (see Fig. 132) but there are many simple methods of making your own. One such method is to draw round an actual object (see Fig. 133). Another very simple method is to use the edge of a sheet of paper as the stencil itself and to move it about as required. Simple shapes of paper, both cut and torn, are very easily adapted to being printed, and the method encourages children to work with large areas of colour. Furthermore, because of the particular process of cutting stencils, ideas become simplified when translated into stencil form. Stencils may be printed by stippling or splattering, in many colours, which may be used at the same time. Although there appears to be a confused splattering on top of the stencil, when it is lifted there is a sharp and clear print (see Fig. 138). This is greatly enjoyed by children.

A number of completely different effects can be made by using various types of inks, different stencils and different colours in the same print (see Figs. 127 and 141). You can also use both the positive and the negative area of the cut-out stencil (see Fig. 131).

By using stencils, it is possible for young children to decorate walls, ceilings, furniture and all kinds of three-dimensional objects very simply and quickly. Flat layers of ink can be printed, and the result will show characteristics quite unlike other methods of printmaking.

Stencil making is also an excellent introduction to silk-screen printing, which is a more complex form of the stencil process.

Left. Fig. 128. Three children stippling on a panoramic print to illustrate the sandy area of a large print.

Right. Fig. 129. 'Horse'.
Tom Anthony, age 5. Cut paper stencil printed with a roller.

A basic reason for using a silk-screen is that 'floating' or loose stencils easily adhere to the screen mesh, and remain in position while being printed. It is also a method of printing more detailed shapes efficiently and easily in large numbers. Involving little expense, it holds great excitement for the imaginative user and is an ideal way of making printed fabrics.

MATERIALS AND TOOLS

General list page 23

Cutting: *scissors, Stanley knife*
Stencils: *tough paper, wax paper, stencil paper, thin cardboard*
Printing: *sponge, gelatine roller, stencil brush, rag*
Inks: *water-based or oil-bound*
Other printing materials: *felt-tipped pens, ball-point pens, paint brushes.*

How to Make Stencils
A stencil is made by cutting, tearing or punching holes into paper or thin cardboard.

The open hole represents the design.

A shaped piece of cardboard or object may be stencilled around.

METHODS OF PRINTING
Once the stencil has been placed on the surface to be printed, several methods can be used to apply the inks:

Stencilling Brush
Load a stiff, short-haired, flat-ended stencil brush with ink and push the ink through the stencil holes, with quick, even stamping.

Textured Stippling
A textured print can be made by using either a textured ink carrier, for example a scrubbing brush, or by placing a rough surface such as

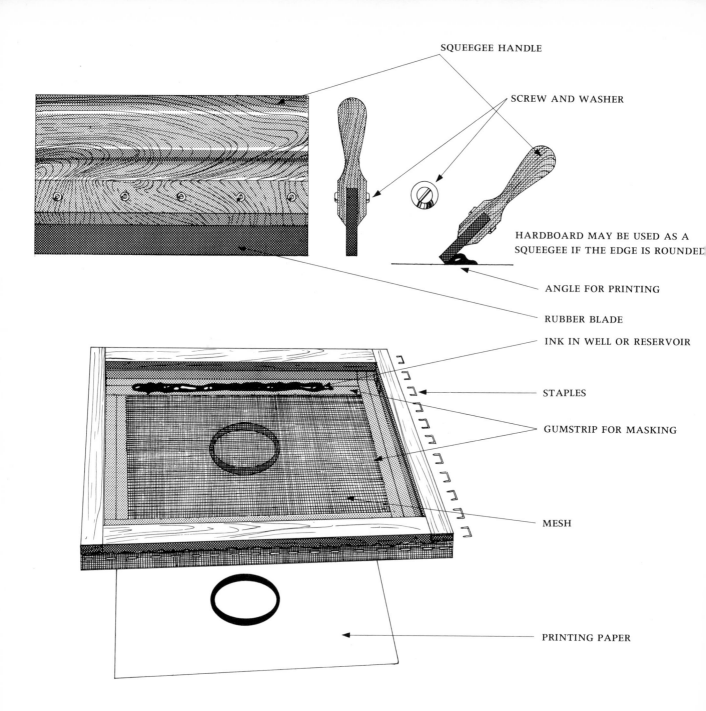

SQUEEGEE HANDLE

SCREW AND WASHER

HARDBOARD MAY BE USED AS A
SQUEEGEE IF THE EDGE IS ROUNDED

ANGLE FOR PRINTING

RUBBER BLADE

INK IN WELL OR RESERVOIR

STAPLES

GUMSTRIP FOR MASKING

MESH

PRINTING PAPER

Left. Fig. 130. Silk-screen and squeegee.

Right. Fig. 131. 'Cows'.
Sonja Hadley, age 10. A simple stencil print of cows made very quickly using both the positive and negative areas of the cut-out stencil, with an ordinary brush and acrylic paint as materials.

sandpaper under the printing paper (see Fig. 103).

Roller Stencilling
Pass an evenly inked roller over the open areas of the stencil. For this method the paper of the stencil must be quite thin, so that the edge of the stencil can be printed crisply and cleanly. It is possible to produce many colours in one printing by having different colours on separate rollers, and printing them through different parts of the stencil.

The stencil should be taped down to the base to prevent the paper sticking to the roller.

SIMPLE SCREEN PRINTING

MATERIALS AND TOOLS
Screen: *wooden frame or sturdy picture frame*
Mesh: *cotton, organdie, silk, net curtains, staples or drawing pins, squeegee, brown tape, sponge and water*
Stencils: *newssheet, newsprint, tracing paper or thin absorbent paper*
Transparent base: *wallpaper paste, or a transparent base can be obtained*
Inks: *fabric dyes, poster paint or powder paint which can be mixed with a base to provide the required colour, specialist inks, either oil- or water-based.*

HOW TO MAKE SIMPLE PAPER STENCILS FOR SILK-SCREEN
Tear or cut out shapes in newsprint, tracing or thin, absorbent paper which has been cut to the outside size of the screen.

PRINTING SILK-SCREEN STENCILS

Make a wooden frame or use a strong picture frame. Stretch the mesh, organdie or silk, tightly over the frame and pin it or staple it tightly in position. Tape all round the sides of the frame and make a well on one side. Put the printing paper on a hard flat base and put the stencil on top. Put the screen in position over the stencil. Pour the ink, which should be fairly thin, into the well and pull it with a squeegee over the surface of the screen. This forces the ink through the screen, which in turn makes the stencil stick to the screen. Those parts of the printing paper not protected by the stencil will be printed. There is a more detailed explanation of screen printing in the second book, *Exploring Printmaking*.

Fig. 132. Number stencil stippled with a brush.

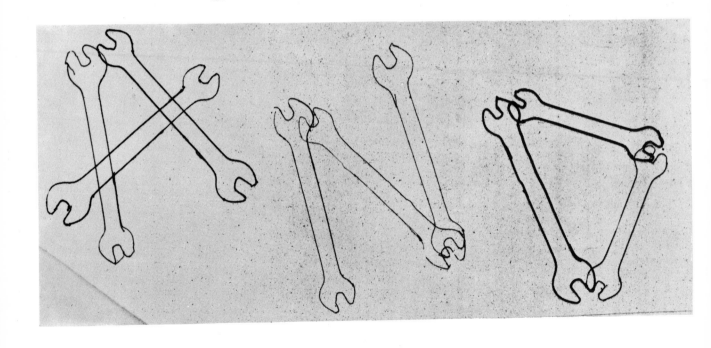

Above. Fig. 133. 'A.N.D.'.
Letters made by using a spanner as stencil.

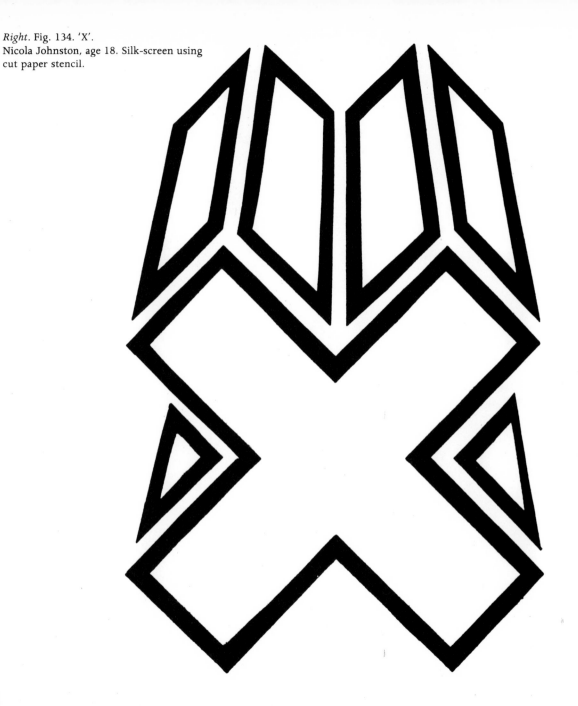

Below. Fig. 135. Stencil letters being printed
with a roller.

Below. Fig. 136. A stencil print of hands
made by holding them over light-sensitive
paper. Compare this with Fig. 138.
(Sussex Association of Youth Clubs. P.H.A.B.
Summer School.)

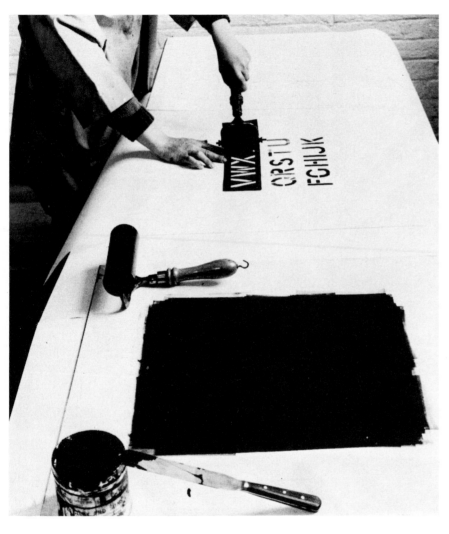

Below. Fig. 135. Stencil letters being printed
with a roller.

Above. Fig. 137. 'Domino Print'.
Chris Fenner, age 14. Cut paper stencil
silk-screen. (Chippenham School. Instructor
Wendy Andrews.)

Left. Fig. 138. Stencil of Hands. A drawing was made around a child's hand. This was then cut out and the open area was used as a stencil with two felt-tipped pens of different colours.

Below. Fig. 139. Commercial stencils used on a packing case.

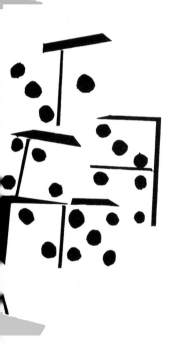

Above. Fig. 140. Football shirts with silk-screen printing.

Left. Fig. 141. 'Bird, Horse and Rider'. Andrea, age 6. Drawing and stencil using felt-tipped pens.

Below. Fig. 142. 'Flags'. Three-dimensional screen print printed in fluorescent colours.

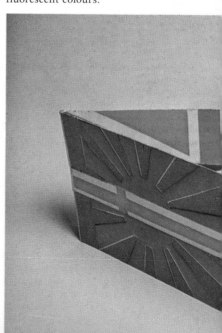

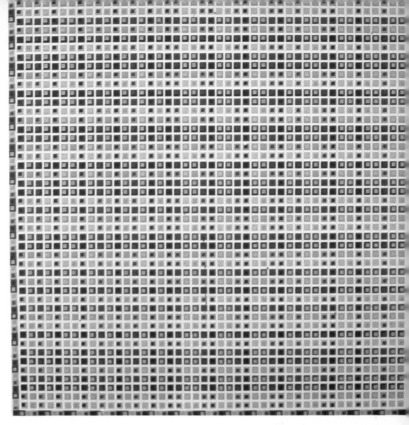

Top left. Fig. 143. 'Clown'.
Henri Matisse, French, 1869–1954. A good
example of a simple silk-screen print. (©
by S.P.A.D.E.M., Paris, 1971. Courtesy
Bibliothèque Nationale, Paris.)

Above. Fig. 144. 'Print Number 27'.
Tony Batchelor. British, born 1944. Silk-
screen.

ACKNOWLEDGEMENTS

Our Thanks go to:

The Museums and Galleries who kindly allowed us to reproduce work from their collections.

The artists who kindly allowed us to reproduce their work.

The teachers who supplied us with work.

Melody Weiler, artist and teacher, who worked so enthusiastically on projects related to the book.

Judy Stapleton, for her work on the manuscript.

Peter Probyn, Art Advisor for East Sussex, for his interest and support and for allowing us to run courses at Lewes Art Centre.

David Smith, who took the photographs.

Those Students of Brighton Polytechnic, Faculty of Art and Design, who worked with us at Lewes and on other courses.

Doug Coupe, art teacher at Imberhorne Comprehensive and those of his pupils who worked with us.

Maurice Barrett, Art Advisor, who let us use work from Redbridge Art Centre.

Bert Latham, for his technical advice and help.

All our Colleagues in the print-making department of Brighton Polytechnic and St. Martin's School of Art, especially Trevor Allen, Selma Nankivell, Peter Hawes, Terry Gravett, Ann d'Arcy Hughes.

Miss Lawson, Head of Tarnerland Nursery School, for her information regarding Pre-School Printmaking.

Chris Swayne, for his general help.

Sigrid Moore, who typed the manuscript.

Tony Truscott, for the illustrations.

The Editors, Anthony Atha and Jean Koefoed.

Printmaking Department, Ohio University, where the Saturday morning classes were held.

All the Schools in Great Britain and U.S.A. who have kindly co-operated in allowing us to work in their classrooms and in giving us information and help.